ME TOO!®
B O O K S

DON'T ROCK THE BOAT!

THE STORY OF THE MIRACULOUS CATCH

By Marilyn Lashbrook

Illustrated by Stephanie McFetridge Britt

RAINBOW
STUDIES
INTERNATIONAL

El Reno, Oklahoma

Creating Colorful Treasures™

Catching fish is man's work;
catching men is God's work. Jesus
showed his disciples how to do
both. DON'T ROCK THE BOAT will
assure your child that God has the
power to care for His little ones and
to help them do great things.

Pretending is a fun way for children
to learn. Pause after questions and
commands to allow your child to
act out rowing, tossing and pulling
in fish nets, and sitting very still.
If it's bed time, act out the
closing poem — following you to
the kitchen for a drink, to the
bathroom to brush teeth and to bed
for prayer and sleep.

As your child grows, let him or her
read beginning words then more
and more of the story to you.
Discuss how God brings blessings
to your child when he or she obeys.

Library of Congress Catalog Card Number: 88-63779
ISBN 0-933657-72-2

Copyright © 1989 and 1998 by Rainbow Studies, Inc.
All rights reserved. Printed in Mexico.

Art direction and design by
Chris Schechner Graphic Design.

1 2 3 4 5 6 7 8 9 — 02 01 00 99 98
Rainbow Studies International, El Reno, OK 73036, U.S.A.

DON'T ROCK THE BOAT!

THE STORY OF THE MIRACULOUS CATCH

Taken from Luke 5

Peter and his friends
had fished all night long,
but they hadn't caught a single fish.

As they rowed their boats to shore,
the colors of the morning sky
danced on the water.

But Peter, James, and John
did not care about the sunrise.
They were tired and grumpy.

(Can you make a grumpy face?)

They climbed out of the boats
and tossed their nets into the water.
It was time
to wash the slippery, slimy seaweed
out of the nets.

*(Can you pretend
you are washing fish nets?)*

Peter spread his nets on the sand
and waited for them to dry.
He was very unhappy
about not catching fish.
He always caught fish!

Then Peter heard someone coming.
He looked up.
There was the Lord Jesus.

Jesus asked Peter to take Him
for a ride in his boat,
and Peter gladly did.

"Throw in your nets," said Jesus.
Peter was surprised!
"We fished all night," he complained,
"and we didn't catch a thing.
But if you say so…"

And Peter obeyed.
*Would you like to pretend
you are Peter throwing the net?*

As soon as the net hit the water,
it was filled with
lots and lots of wiggly fish.

"Hurry!" Peter yelled,
"Bring the other boat!"

James and John jumped into their boat
and rowed as fast as they could!
Splish-splash, splish-splash, splish-splash!

Peter and his friends
tugged and tugged.

(Can you help pull in the nets?)

"Oh, these fish are
so heavy!" they laughed.
Now, they were very happy!

The men pulled in so many fish
that their boats could barely float!

(Sit very still! Don't rock the boat!)

Peter and his friends
rowed s-l-o-w-l-y back to shore.
They had NEVER had a catch
like this before.

Peter was amazed.
Only God could have brought
that many fish into their nets.
It was wonderful
to go fishing with Jesus!

But Jesus told him
there was something better
than catching a lot of fish.

"Follow me," Jesus said.
"I will make you fishers of men."

Peter, James and John
left their nets
and followed Jesus.

We want to fish for men.
  (clap, clap)
And snatch them out of sin.
  (clap, clap)
We'll talk of God's love,
And Heaven above.
We want to fish for men.
  (clap, clap)

ME TOO!®
B O O K S

Ages 2-7

SOMEONE TO LOVE
THE STORY OF CREATION

TWO BY TWO
THE STORY OF NOAH'S FAITH

I DON'T WANT TO
THE STORY OF JONAH

I MAY BE LITTLE
THE STORY OF DAVID'S GROWTH

I'LL PRAY ANYWAY
THE STORY OF DANIEL

WHO NEEDS A BOAT?
THE STORY OF MOSES

GET LOST, LITTLE BROTHER
THE STORY OF JOSEPH

THE WALL THAT DID NOT FALL
THE STORY OF RAHAB'S FAITH

NO TREE FOR CHRISTMAS
THE STORY OF JESUS' BIRTH

NOW I SEE
THE STORY OF THE MAN BORN BLIND

DON'T ROCK THE BOAT!
THE STORY OF THE MIRACULOUS CATC

OUT ON A LIMB
THE STORY OF ZACCHAEUS

SOWING AND GROWING
THE PARABLE OF THE SOWER AND THE S

DON'T STOP. . . FILL EVERY POT
THE STORY OF THE WIDOW'S OIL

GOOD, BETTER, BEST
THE STORY OF MARY AND MARTHA

GOD'S HAPPY HELPERS
THE STORY OF TABITHA AND FRIEND

Ages 5-10

IT'S NOT MY FAULT
MAN'S BIG MISTAKE

GOD, PLEASE SEND FIRE!
ELIJAH AND THE
PROPHETS OF BAAL

TOO BAD, AHAB
NABOTH'S VINEYARD

THE WEAK STRONGMAN
SAMSON

NOTHING TO FEAR
JESUS WALKS ON WATER

THE BEST DAY EVER
THE STORY OF JESUS

THE GREAT SHAKE-UP
MIRACLES IN PHILIPPI

TWO LADS AND A DAD
THE PRODIGAL SON

NOBODY KNEW BUT C
MIRIAM AND BABY MOS

MORE THAN BEAUTI
THE STORY OF ESTHER

FAITH TO FIGHT
THE STORY OF CALEB

BIG ENEMY, BIGGER C
THE STORY OF GIDEON

WE SEE!™
V I D E O S

VIDEOS FOR TODAY'S CHRISTIAN FAMILY.
51 animated Bible stories from the Old Testament ("In the Beginning" Series) and New Testament ("A Kingdom without Fronti
Series) will provide your children with a solid cornerstone of spiritual support.

Available at your local bookstore or from:

Rainbow Studies International

P.O. Box 759 • El Reno, Oklahoma 73036 • 1-800-242-5348

RSI
Creating Colorful Trea